A Manual

for

Documentation

Fieldwork

&

Preservation

for

Ethnomusicologists

For addional copies of *A Manual for Documentation, Fieldwork & Preservation for Ethnomusicologists*, contact:

THE SOCIETY FOR ETHNOMUSICOLOGY
Morrison Hall, Room 005
Indiana University
Bloomington IN 47405

Tel. (812) 855-6672
Fax (812) 855-6673
sem@indiana.edu
www.ethnomusicology.org

CONTENTS

Acknowledgements

This publication, the product of many years work, has been prepared with the help of members of the Society for Ethnomusicology Archiving Committee. Over the years, the membership of the committee has changed, but we would especially like to acknowledge the contributions of the following people to this project: Anthony Seeger, Louise Spear, Suzanne Flandreau, Judith Gray, Mark Forry, Nora Dial, Shubha Chaudhuri, Randy Baier, and Marcia Maguire. Nan McEntire, Rick Faris, and Heather Shupp helped with the first edition, upon which this new edition is largely based. We also gratefully acknowledge the assistance of the Center for Folklife Programs and Cultural Studies, and especially Joan Wolbier, for design of the first edition.

For revision and production of this second edition, we thank Janet Topp Fargion, Alan Burdette, Joe Ellison, Laurel Sercombe, Jennifer Post, Ginny Danielson, Marilyn Graf, Patrick Feaster, and John Fenn. We would also like to acknowledge the resources of the Archives of Traditional Music as well as the Sound and Video Analysis and Instruction Laboratory (SAVAIL) at Indiana University.

Introduction

Ethnomusicologists are part of a process whereby musical traditions all over the world are recorded, documented, studied, written about, and made accessible to new audiences. We are not the only people doing this, but our goals are scholarship and understanding, and the time frame within which we should be thinking is longer than that of most other people carrying recorders and talking about music. The results of our work are often useful and sometimes highly significant to the peoples whose music we have studied—sometimes decades after we made the recordings. Furthermore, as ethnomusicologists, we have obligations not only to ourselves and to our institutions, but to the traditions we study and the people from whom we learn.

The authors of this manual have done fieldwork, worked in archives, and talked with researchers, community representatives and other patrons about ethnomusicology. We know that the topics covered here are only a small part of the preparation for a good fieldwork project—but we also know from long experience how often ethnomusicologists and communities have regretted their inattention to these issues.

We have compiled this guide to facilitate the effective collection and preservation of all kinds of data. It is meant to supplement, not replace, other works on fieldwork, and has been produced in a form compact enough to be taken to the field. We pose questions and propose alternatives rather than dictate firm recommendations, because objectives differ and technology will change. We recommend how to document and preserve your field data in order to assure their usefulness in the future. This doesn't mean this is all you should do. But, if you carefully include this information, your data will have a longer "shelf life," far beyond the seemingly vivid recollections in your mind. We want your materials to travel safely, to be useful, and to remain in good condition for many years.

A great deal happens in field research, and it is often difficult to keep common sense guidelines in mind. Experienced fieldworkers know that a little time taken to write down a performer's name and address carefully, or to get the local terms for a performance genre, can prevent confusion or misunderstanding later. Effective documentation can make data valuable not only for the researcher returning from the field with a large body of information to organize, analyze, and interpret, but also for future generations of scholars.

For most ethnomusicologists—whether students, teachers, performers, or researchers—the purpose of recording field data is to study and preserve musical traditions. Each item in a field collection is a valuable document. Fieldworkers do not always appreciate an item's value at the time, but they should assume that whatever is gathered will be of importance to them and to other scholars, or to members of the communities where the recordings were made, at some time in the future.

This manual is organized into five chapters, each containing information on an aspect of fieldwork that affects fieldworkers, informants, archives, and future researchers. Topics include documenting fieldwork, ethical and legal issues, selecting recording equipment, recording procedures, and storing and preserving archival materials. Where possible we have provided further references in the form of books, articles and stable websites.

We hope you will find this publication a useful accessory to your field study.

I.
Documentation

Accompanying documentation is as important as the recording itself, since the nature and content of recordings are not always self-evident. A recording without documentation cannot be cataloged by an archivist or effectively utilized by any future researcher. This section focuses specifically on documentation other than the recording itself; that is, "all information which purports to identify or make fully comprehensible the event(s) captured on a field recording" (Ward 1990:244). This includes data on both the physical characteristics and the intellectual content of the collection. In addition to index sheets, such things as film, photos, slides, field notes, transcriptions, manuscripts, programs, and computer disks may all serve as documentation.

Organizing documentation
Documentation for field recordings may consist of a great diversity of data. The collector has unlimited freedom in choosing the degree of detail and the format for arranging these data and should set aside time for planning this aspect of the field trip. Each research project is unique, so what follows is a general outline of possible questions, issues, and types of data that might be useful in documenting your collection. Take the time to evaluate your particular field situation and equipment, and

I

generate a documentation system that fits your collection. Also, it is a good idea to contact an archive before conducting fieldwork, as they will be able to provide guidelines for documentation. Creating a ready-to-use form can save you time in the field and can be an encouragement to complete what are essential, but admittedly tedious, parts of the research process.

Numbering materials

Written documentation is only useful when connected to the appropriate physical item (tape, film, etc.), and the unit within that item (song, photo, etc.). In order to insure effectiveness of such documentation, each physical item must be consecutively numbered, preferably before going to the field. Tapes and their containers should be numbered. Rolls of film may be numbered with tape or other labels, and ideally the first frame should be a shot of the roll number.

Documentation must match the units making up the item. This may be accomplished by using an index sheet for each physical item. For example, on an index sheet for cassette tape #7, each song or section should be numbered and identified by title and as many of the elements listed below as possible. For a videotape, the index sheet could indicate each new scene, location, performer, or setting for a continuous event. Since every project is unique, index sheets should be designed specifically to accommodate your research. Again, consulting with an archive beforehand will help guide you in this step.

Examples of data to be collected for every recording

Event (musical event or interview)
- Date: year, month, day, time, local calendar (if applicable)
- Place: country, state/region, city/town/village/ address
- Name/title of event
- Participants: estimated or exact numbers
- Instruments used
  — Name (indigenous and English equivalent)
  — Number of each instrument
  — Local and Sachs-Hornbostel classification
  — Ensemble formation
- Culture groups
- Audience: size, makeup, role in event
- Context: social circumstances surrounding event, history, etc.
- Purpose/ reason for event
- Possible ethical considerations for future use of data

Performer(s)/performing group/informant/ consultant
- Name and address: surname, given name, nickname, title, contact info
- Role/function at event: i.e., guitarist, dancer, consultant
- Age: exact or approximation
- Gender
- Language(s) used in event

I

- Culture group/ ethnic identity
- Religious identification (if relevant to event)
- Biographical information

Data to be collected about the media—*provide thorough information about the kind of equipment and media used, including all settings, speeds, and other variables.*

Audio and video recordings
- Format: mono, stereo, or multitrack? Digital or analog? NTSC, PAL, or SECAM?
- Recording speed
  —Audio: tape speed (analog)
           sampling rate (digital)
  —Video: SP, LP, or SLP?
- Size of media: tape width and length
- Generation: original, first-generation copy, or subsequent copy?
- Enhancements/alterations: noise reduction (Dolby or other)? Filters? Overdubs?
- Duration: days, hours, minutes, seconds
- Recorder: brand name, model number
- Tape: brand name, characteristics
- Microphone: brand name, model number, omni- or unidirectional
- Number of microphones and placement (diagram is helpful)
- Acoustics: general observations, special conditions (e.g., use of amplification), problems

Film (motion picture)
- Color or black-and-white?
- Sound: silent or synchronized?
- Number of feet
- Width: 8mm or 16mm
- Generation: original or copy?
- Camera: brand name and model number

Photographs/slides
- Color or black-and-white?
- Camera: brand name and model number
- Film: brand name and speed
- Accessories: type of filters, flash, etc.
- Camera settings: f-stop, exposure time, lens focal length
- Contact sheets (especially useful for shot sequences)

Information about the collector

- Name and address: current postal/email addresses, telephone number
- Institutional affiliation
- Signed forms/releases
- Purpose of project
- Funding received/sponsors
- Other institutions involved
- Other fieldworkers/researchers involved
- Recording engineer(s) involved

Associated materials

- Field notes
  - Identify each page with your name and a page number
  - Write legibly or type
- Transcription/translations (related to specific tape and item)
- Programs/ephemera/publications
  - Relate to specific item(s) in collection
- Computer disks
  - Name and model of computer used
  - Name and release of software

I

II.
Ethical and Legal Considerations

Ethics

The Society for Ethnomusicology's statement of *Ethical Considerations* is published as an appendix to this manual. This chapter reflects the perspectives of practicing ethnomusicologists as they relate specifically to fieldwork. As a field researcher, you are the best-qualified person to make ethical decisions regarding your recordings, photographs, and other documentation gathered in the field. You know the facts and the nuances of your field environment well enough to respect differences in perspectives, the social and political expectations that influence your behavior, the sensitive areas in the lives of your informants, and your own motivations and expectations for your work.

Though each field situation is unique, some principles of responsible field research should be considered in all situations:

You are responsible for your conduct in the field. Whatever the role of your university, your faculty advisor, your colleagues, your granting agency, or your government, you and your work will be judged by the ethical behavior as well as the intellectual rigor you exhibit.

Represent yourself honestly. It is unacceptable to misrepresent your reasons for being present in a community or to record your informants without their knowledge. Apply the concept of informed consent to all your dealings with your informants.

Confidentiality is basic to all research involving human beings. Building trust with your informants is, of course, one of your main tasks. You may have to make tough decisions, based on the wishes of your informants or their families or some other influential person or group in the community, not only about what can be recorded or photographed, but about possible restrictions placed on the use of the material. You should also be aware of possible claims by national agencies.

Respect your informants' beliefs and traditions. You may object to attitudes or behaviors on a personal level, but in your role as researcher, do not pass judgment.

Be aware of proprietary concerns. Among those who may have a sense of ownership of recorded materials are those recorded, their families and descendants, members of the source culture, collectors' families and descendants, archives, archives users, archivists, funding agencies, and governments. Those concerned may coexist successfully or not. You, as collector, can minimize conflict by openly stating your role and purpose, by obtaining written or recorded permission from your informants for all recording, filming, and photography, and by fulfilling promptly any post-field agreement you have made.

Economic concerns and proprietary concerns often go together. When economic gain, or an appearance thereof, is at stake, ownership of taped material may take on new meaning. A discussion of copyright and its role appears later in this chapter. Again, negotiating mutually satisfactory agreements is the best precaution you can take to avoid being misunderstood later.

Cultivate honest relationships with your colleagues, respecting research in progress and avoiding secrecy about your own work. Should other researchers be in the area, work with them to set up a situation you are each agreeable to, and one that does not cause tension or conflict with any of your informants or partners.

Many ethical dilemmas arise because two or more ethical principles or systems clash. As a field researcher, you may want to record material that is considered by your informants too sacred, personally meaningful, or even shameful to commit to tape. You may be able to provide reassurances against misuse of the material, but in the end you will have to respect their wishes or risk jeopardizing the integrity of your relationship. If you receive permission to record on the condition that access to part or all of the recording be restricted, suggest a time limit on these restrictions.

Legal considerations

This discussion on legal matters, specifically copyright and privacy as they pertain to ethnomusicological fieldwork, is intended to inform

II

you about the issues and problems involved. It is not intended to substitute for advice by a qualified attorney.

Copyright

This manual is published in the United States. It is assumed that its intended audience is based primarily in the United States and that most field collections created by the users of this manual will find their way into archives in the United States as well as archives in the country of origin. Therefore, this manual stresses United States law. Every country has its own copyright laws. You are responsible for knowing the laws of the countries in which you conduct research.

Laws governing intellectual property are constantly changing, through legislation and through interpretation by the courts, both of which are expanding the areas covered by the law. You should not rely on Federal copyright legislation to provide unambiguous answers to your questions about copyright protection for field recordings. Until the courts are called upon to provide interpretations of the law in such cases, the current professional standards of ethical field conduct are your best guide.

The purpose of copyright is to promote creative expression by protecting the right of authors and creators to benefit from the sale of their works. Copyright does not protect facts or ideas, only the expression of facts or ideas. Provision for copyright legislation is made in Article I, Section 8 of the United States Constitution, which grants Congress the power to protect artistic expression. The copyright law is Title 17 of the U.S. Code. It was last completely rewritten and passed in 1976, took effect in 1978, and has been amended by Congress many times since then. The latest additions, in 1998, extended the term of copyright. In addition Congress made provision for protection of new forms of digitized copyrighted material through the Digital Millennium Copyright Act.

II

Current copyright covers published and unpublished works equally and allows a copyright to exist in a work from the moment the work itself exists in a fixed form (a written document, recording, photograph, video recording, etc.). The owner of a copyrighted work has the exclusive right to make and distribute copies of the work. Copyright is a property right: it can be bought and sold, transferred, and licensed, like any other tangible property. The concept of copyright is essentially a business concept, intended to allow copyright owners to profit from their works for a fixed period of time. It does not take into account community ownership of indigenous material, spirit authorship, or other more traditional concepts a researcher may encounter. If you wish to protect the rights of your informants, you may need to convince individuals or representative bodies to allow you to act as a copyright agent, or to act as agents themselves to protect their interests.

The 1976 copyright law does not require registration as a prerequisite to copyright protection. However, works must be registered before litigation can occur. If you believe that your copyrights have

II

been infringed, you should consult an attorney. Field notes, release forms, and other documentation you can provide may then become important in the outcome of any litigation.

Multiple copyrights may exist for a single work. For example, if you make a recording of a song, you own the copyright for that particular sound recording as soon as the recording is fixed, but others may own the copyright to the underlying work. Copyright in a recording is based on the creative process of recording, for example, mixing levels or track selection. In addition, different creators may hold copyright separately in the music and lyrics to a song. In interviews, which can be considered works of joint or multiple authorship, each speaker owns the rights to his or her own expression. Before any use other than your own private study can be made of the recording each of these levels of ownership must be addressed.

Copyright ownership is not perpetual; it exists for a limited duration. The term of copyright under the 1976 law as amended in 1998 is the life of an individual author plus 70 years. For works of joint authorship it is the life of the last surviving author plus 70 years. Works of corporate authorship (called "works for hire" in the law) have a term of copyright of 95 years for published works and 120 years for unpublished works. For works published and copyrighted before 1978, the term of copyright is 95 years from the date of publication. Though traditional informants may feel that their cultural heritage is owned by the group forever, the copyright law does not protect their ownership to that extent. Most existing copyrights will terminate many years in the future, but you should be aware, and make your informants aware, that under United States law copyright ownership does not confer perpetual rights.

The 1976 copyright law extends the protection of United States law to works copyrighted in countries with reciprocal agreements with the United states, and to all unpublished material, no matter where the author or creator resides. If you intend to do fieldwork outside the United States, you should be aware of the copyright laws for that country and of any reciprocal agreements with the United States. Some countries have also included protection of traditional music in copyright legislation, as part of their national heritage, although United States law does not.

In the United States the music industry has developed a complex system of licenses and royalties that allows copyright owners to collect compensation due to them for performance or recording of their music. Rights organizations such as ASCAP, BMI, and SESAC distribute royalties to their members. If you intend to study any form of popular music that is published, commercially recorded, or sold, you should be aware of the policies of local rights organizations, because you may later need to deal with them for permission to publish transcriptions or recordings.

The 1976 copyright act did not provide for a right of performance; a performer could not automatically expect royalties unless he or she also held authorship

II

in the work. However, in 1994, Congress recognized some rights of performers in Section 1101: "Unauthorized fixation and trafficking in sound recordings and music videos." Though the provision is intended as an anti-piracy statement aimed at those who make and sell unauthorized copies of commercial releases, the language of the law is not limited to commercial settings and would cover scholarly products, not-for-profit enterprises, and other recording situations. The law states:

> "Anyone who, without the consent of the performer or performers involved 1) fixes the sounds or sounds and images of a live musical performance in a copy or phonorecord, or reproduces copies or phonorecords of such a performance from an unauthorized fixation, 2) transmits or otherwise communicates to the public the sounds or sounds and images of a live musical performance, or 3) distributes or offers to distribute, sells or offers to sell, rents or offers to rent, or traffics in any copy or phonorecord fixed as described [above], regardless of whether the fixations occurred in the United States, shall be subject to the remedies provided in sections 502 through 505, to the same extent as an infringer of copyright."

Sections 501-505 define willful copyright infringement as a criminal act and list as remedies impoundment and possible forfeiture and destruction of the infringing material, actual and statutory damages, court costs and attorneys' fees. The law directly reinforces the ethnomusicologist's ethical obligations to informants. Permission, either obtained verbally and recorded at the beginning of a session, or in writing, must be obtained before a recording is made.

For more information on copyright on an international scale consult the following sources:

The World Intellectual Property Organization. *Introduction to Intellectual Property Theory and Practice*. London, The Hague, Boston: Kluwer International, 1997.

Sinacore-Guinn, David. *Collective Administration of Copyright and Neighbouring Rights: International Practices, Procedures, and Organizations*. Boston, Toronto, London: Little, Brown and Company, 1993.

Stewart, Stephen M. *International Copyright and Neighbouring Rights*. London, Boston, Dublin, etc.: Butterworth's, 1993.

II

Privacy considerations

A distinction should be made between copyright ownership and an individual's right to privacy. Unlike copyright, growing concerns about privacy have been addressed by individual state laws rather than by one comprehensive federal law. The right of publicity is the right of an individual to control and prevent commercial exploitation of his or her name, likeness, and personal information. Though enforcement of the right of publicity through litigation depends on the laws of an individual's place of residence, a publisher may expect clearances that cover the entire distribution area of a work that features that person. Ethnomusicologists should be aware of this growing

II

legal trend. It may be advisable to obtain from an informant authorization in writing to make use of his or her name, likeness, biographical data, and voice for academic and commercial purposes, including a dissertation or thesis and derived publications. This license should not be exclusive, but limited to the particular project and any resulting products. Such a license can be incorporated into a permission form.

Permissions and other documentation

Consult the archives where you plan to deposit your collection to find out their requirements for deposit. Most archives will ask for a description of your agreements with informants. Some may refuse to accept collections without evidence that the rights of informants have been respected in the course of field study. In the event that you may at some later date publish some of your recordings, you should make such provisions in your deposit agreement.

Determine before going into the field what the probable uses of your field material will be. It is your responsibility to communicate the purpose of your research and the expected results to your informants. If your recordings and other field documentation are to be source material for a dissertation, and the eventual publication of a book, article, or recording is likely, you will need to consider the possibility of compensating your informants in some way for their services. Most book and audiovisual publishers require an author to obtain permissions and to accept legal responsibility if a lawsuit should result from publication of field materials.

Because you cannot know the reactions of people ahead of time, you should be prepared to be flexible. Many musicians are willing to cooperate with a project they understand is for educational purposes, but attitudes may be different if there is the perception that you stand to profit financially from your research. Many field researchers show their appreciation to those they work with by purchasing gifts or providing assistance to individuals or families. The trust that develops as you spend time in any given community goes both ways; you are the best judge of what is appropriate to ask of those with whom you work, as well as what to offer in return.

II

Prepare recording agreement forms or develop a format for recording permissions. You may obtain permission in writing or verbally (with the tape recorder running), but it's best to keep written records of these transactions in either case.

Anticipate situations in which you may need to be particularly sensitive to community concerns. Consult the literature in your research areas as well as your advisors and colleagues whose experience may be instructive. Also, locate at least one project adviser whose judgment you trust and who is willing to be called upon while you are in the field if you should encounter a tricky ethical dilemma.

In the field, keep a daily log detailing your interactions with informants. Include mention of formal and informal discussions, agreements, conflicts, and resolutions of conflicts.

II

It may also be advisable, especially if you work with elderly informants, to obtain the name and address of a family member or other individual designated to act as the informant's heir or agent in future contacts.

Keep in mind, also, especially if you intend to work with popular musicians, that they may not own the copyrights to the music they perform, and that your permission form will cover only their interviews and performances and their personal information. You will need to obtain clearances or licenses to quote from or publish the music itself from the actual copyright owners.

When negotiating with informants, the only ethical course is to be honest about the possible consequences of your work. Keep them informed about changes in your work that may affect them; don't risk their hearing potentially upsetting news from someone else.

Finally, following your fieldwork period, fulfill all obligations to your informants as quickly as possible. Honor any promises you make regarding copies of fieldtapes, transcriptions of interviews, photographic prints, or duplicates of publications using your data.

Permission forms

A written permission form should be tailored to the individual fieldwork situation, including, if necessary, translation into the appropriate language. Keep in mind that literacy is not always a standard, so permission should also be recorded on audio or video tape if possible.

A permission form should document the following:

- Place, date, and time of recording

- Name and address of informant

- The event to be recorded and the informant's authority to represent the community or group being recorded (if necessary)

- The use that will be made of the recording including:

    a. Academic study: e.g. quotation or transcription in an academic dissertation or thesis

    b. Quotation or transcription in any derived publications

    c. Any possible academic or commercial issue of the sound recording

    d. Deposit of originals or copies in an archival repository

- A statement authorizing you to use an informant's likeness, name, biographical information, and voice, in both academic and commercial products.

The permission agreement can also include any promises you have made to your informants, including making copies of recordings for the informant or the community, and where such copies are to be sent, sharing of potential royalties, or similar matters of concern to the informant.

23

III.
Recording Equipment, Photographic Equipment, and Accessories

Planning for the field involves correlating your research objectives with the equipment that will best fulfill them. The decisions you make about equipment for fieldwork will affect the quality and accessibility of the field materials you produce. Purchasing the best digital setup on the market will not necessarily make you a better researcher, but with careful use of currently available equipment all field workers can expect to make good recordings that effectively document musical events.

You will almost always have to balance considerations of expense and quality. Try to obtain a flexible system with sufficient accessories. The quality of your field recordings, though, will only be as good as the lowest quality component in your recording system. This chapter covers some questions, issues, and topics you should consider while gathering equipment for your field research.

Before you begin

Determine what your immediate documentation needs will be. Think about the kinds of things you want to record and why. Outlining your needs beforehand will help you determine the kinds of equipment that will fit your budget. Ask yourself questions regarding:

The nature of your research objectives

- What musical activities do you need to document?
- What kinds of data will you collect? Visual and/or aural? Music and/or spoken word?
- How complete a contextual picture will you need?
- Do you need to isolate song texts from surrounding sounds?
- Do you need to capture a full range of festival activity?

Intended uses of your recorded materials

- Will your recordings serve primarily as source material for your own research, or others' research also?
- What kind of audio/visual data is going to best answer your research questions?
- Do you plan to publish or broadcast recordings? Commercial or educational distribution?
- Will you use your recordings in teaching? Do you intend to return copies of recordings to the source community?

Field conditions

- Will you be working alone or with others? Will you be physically isolated?
- How intrusive is your presence likely to be?
- Over what kind of terrain will you need to walk/travel with your equipment?

- Will you be able to mail or ship your materials from your field site?
- Where will you have to travel for equipment repairs?
- What will your recording environment be like? Indoor/outdoor recording? Daytime or nighttime? Controlled/uncontrolled recording environment? What power will be available? Weather conditions (humidity; day/night temperature difference)? Political considerations (permission for recording; knowledge of jurisdictions; safety; ease of departure from area)? Local laws regarding recording or photographing in public areas?
- How much technical knowledge do you possess about audio, video, and photography? Are you confident operating the equipment you will bring with you?

Also consider what you might want to document beyond your immediate research needs. You may have to forego such extras for the sake of economics or portability, but considering possible future projects or extensions of your current research may help you choose between two similar models or may spread the usefulness of your investment over five years instead of one.

Obtaining equipment

Purchasing or borrowing

Some universities and research institutions lend recording equipment to fieldworkers. Short-term loans may not help you for an extended overseas fieldwork trip, but they may be just what you need for fieldwork close to home. Also, using borrowed equipment is likely to help you decide what you like and dislike before you purchase equipment for yourself.

Long-term loans may be available, but before you enter into an agreement, make sure the equipment is in good condition and has been well maintained. Test the equipment thoroughly before you use it for your research, and find out if there will be someone you can contact if you experience difficulties in the field.

Keeping up with the market

The models that are available for purchase in each format change constantly. It is easy to find out what is new in audio and video technologies by regularly consulting *High Fidelity*, *Stereo Review*, *Audiophile*, *Camcorder*, *Videomaker*, and other print publications devoted to the consumer market. The World Wide Web is also a good source for information. Sites such as *www.solorb.com/dat-heads/* (information on DAT), *www.minidisc.org/* (information on minidisc), and *www.imaging-resource.com* (information on digital photography) offer tips on evaluating, buying, and using the latest recording devices. Many of the "user group" sites also have FAQs (archives of Frequently Asked Questions) that can get you started with an unfamiliar format.

As with so much else in fieldwork, your ability to get information about equipment depends on making useful contacts. An audio technician can help to evaluate equipment options and answer questions about appropriate cables, microphones, compatibility of components, and powering equipment, especially if you are not conversant with all the technical aspects of recording. Increasingly, this type of information is widely available on the Web, provided you have a firm idea of what you want to know. The Web will most likely contain information that can help you in making decisions—or at least formulating new questions—but rarely will it provide you with the perfect equipment solution. Instead, use the Web to gather details and opinions about the equipment you are considering, then make an informed choice. And do not forget to get advice and input from teachers and colleagues in ethnomusicology, anthropology, and folklore; their experience can be invaluable.

III

Consumer, prosumer, and professional

While contemplating your options for equipment, you may encounter distinctions in catalogs or product literature between consumer, prosumer, and professional equipment. These terms refer to different levels of features, expense, and quality. Consumer-level equipment is widely available and affordable, while professional equipment is much more expensive and usually found in specialty catalogs and shops. Prosumer equipment falls in between the two, and commonly has features associated with professional gear but at consumer-level prices. Remember that higher-priced equipment does not always guarantee higher-quality recordings or more dependability in the field, but it does tend to give you more features that allow greater control over the final product.

Audio versus video

The decision about whether you use audio or video recording equipment must be made based on the nature of your research, but consider that a video camera may be able to perform double duty. Today's digital video cameras are capable of making very high quality audio recordings. The blank media may be more expensive, but you may save the weight and expense of another recording device. On the other hand, even if you decide to utilize video equipment you may also want to carry a compact audiocassette recorder to the field for interviews or situations where video recording would be inappropriate. A cassette recorder is also useful for recording your own observations and notes.

Digital versus analog

Digital and analog are two fundamentally different ways of capturing audio and visual information for storage and playback. Each has its advantages and disadvantages and choosing between them will be one of your first decisions.

In analog recording the sound signal is picked up by the microphone, converted into an electrical signal, amplified, and sent to the record head on the recorder, which converts it to a signal configured as a magnetic pattern on a strip of plastic tape. During playback the original sound is reproduced as recorded

III

when the magnetic pattern is read by the playback head, converted back to an electrical signal, and amplified.

Accompanying the intentionally recorded signal is the electronic and mechanical noise created by the tape recorder itself and additional noise present on all magnetic tape, even when new. High-quality equipment and the use of noise reduction devices cut down—but do not eliminate—unwanted noise that contaminates analog recordings. As a tape is copied and that copy copied, noise and distortion increase until "generation loss" is such that tape noise begins to interfere seriously with the clarity of the recording.

Digital recording uses a different process. The sound signal picked up by the microphone is converted into an electrical signal and then encoded as a series of numbers stored in the form of magnetic pulses on a plastic tape (or coded optically on a disc). The encoded series of numbers are referred to as "samples," and the number of samples taken per minute is the "sampling rate"; 44.1 kHz and 48 kHz are common rates. The coding process is referred to as Pulse Code Modulation (PCM), and practically all current digital formats use it. Noise inherent to analog recording equipment is eliminated altogether (though digital systems are not completely without noise or distortion), and copies of digital recordings can be made that are essentially identical to the original.

Many specialists feel strongly about the superior quality of digital recording over high-quality analog

III

recording, but the latter also has its defenders. The advantages of digital recordings of music are the extremely wide dynamic range, virtual absence of noise, very wide and flat frequency response, and low distortion. Problems associated with early digital recordings include the tendency for distortion at low levels and a lack of a sense of ambience or spaciousness. These problems have been minimized in newer equipment. However, supporters of analog recordings argue that they are "warmer" or more natural sounding than digital, and that standard digital sampling rates do not accurately reproduce high frequencies. You must be your own judge.

Preservation and performance are two additional criteria to consider before deciding on a recording system. Digital Audio Tape (DAT) is still relatively new, and we know less about its behavior as a storage medium than we do about analog tape. In general, DAT has not demonstrated the same longevity as analog tape, and archivists do not consider it a satisfactory preservation medium at this time. Humidity appears to be a significant hazard with DAT recordings and equipment, a factor that should be seriously considered before purchasing equipment for field research.

Input level controls

In many field recording situations, you must control the input level of the audio signal. For example, if you are recording an outdoor festival, constant loud noises may distort the overall recording and render it useless. Or a person you are interviewing may speak softly and you will need to increase the sensitivity (or gain) of your recording gear, whether it is audio or video. With professional gear this is usually possible, but with much consumer gear it is not (prosumer gear falls in the middle).

If you can adjust the recording or input level, often there will be some way for you to monitor or measure that level. A "VU meter" is the most common method for measuring the loudness of sounds, and these are often built into tape decks or high-end video cameras. They may have needles that measure the levels, or a series of LED lights. What these measure is referred to as "dbv" or decibles against voltage. VU meters do not respond quickly to short bursts of loud sound, which may cause brief distortion or overload of your recording gear ("peaking"). A peak meter allows you to monitor such short bursts, usually in the form of a blinking red light. However, peak meters are not as suitable for monitoring normal levels of sound over long periods of time, and so the ideal situation is to have both.

Distortion in analog systems gradually increases as the level approaches or exceeds the 0 dbv level. In digital recording, however, distortion actually decreases the closer you get to 0 dbv, but you never want to go beyond the 0 dbv level because once you cross that line, your audio signal is completely ruined. "Clipping" (or "clipping the preamp") refers to a signal that is too strong for the equipment to handle, thus turning your original signal into a sound with very unpleasant noise and distortion.

III

Automatic Gain Control (AGC) systems are designed to make setting levels foolproof, but they rarely work very well. If you are working alone, they have the advantage of freeing up your attention to the interview or event at hand. However, you will often trade this for issues of audio quality. AGC typically appears on consumer level equipment and is generally not very good. The two main problems with AGC are:

1. It does not respond quickly enough to short loud sounds and so they clip anyway.
2. Short loud sounds (like a cough), reset the gain to a lower level and then it gradually comes up.

If someone is talking and there are silent pauses, the gain (and the ambient sound level) will go up, before decreasing when they resume talking. The result is called "pumping" or "breathing" and it can sound like an audio roller coaster as the ambient noise continually rises and falls. Almost all consumer and prosumer video recorders have AGC systems built in, which you often cannot turn off. Prosumer equipment may have more sophisticated AGC systems, however, and they may also allow you to switch to a manual mode.

Choosing blank media

This guide addresses the pros and cons of various recording devices in more detail below, but as you choose equipment you will need to figure the characteristics of the blank media into the complex equation of what to buy. Important issues include cost, weight, size, availability (at home and in the field), recording duration, potential quality, and archival life. You will likely make some compromises based on what is most important to you. For example, you may choose the quality and compact size of DAT over its short archival life, high cost, and limited availability. Make yourself aware of all the issues surrounding particular media, and consider them in making your choice.

For the most part, field recording equipment is primarily tape-based (with disc-based systems like MiniDisc being a current exception). Analog audio, digital audio, and video cameras all rely on cassettes of some sort that house plastic tape coated with a thin layer of magnetized metallic particles designed to store the encoded audio or visual data. Choosing blank media for your recording setup can be just as important as choosing equipment. While each format and media type carries specific concerns, there are some general issues to consider when purchasing blank media for your equipment.

First, with magnetic tapes longer recording times usually indicate thinner tape stock, which may lead to stretching or breaking of the tape. Adjustable recording rates on the equipment may also produce longer recording times on a given cassette, but this is related to the speed with which the tape moves over the recording heads rather than the physical length of the tape. In general, it is advisable to use shorter tapes to avoid any problems. Check manufacturer specifications and consult with others who have used similar equipment to get a better idea

III

in your particular case. And keep in mind that many professional video playback decks will not even play tapes recorded in "long play" or LP mode.

Second, while popular brand names may be more expensive (Maxell, TDK, Sony), they are also proven and reliable. However, this does not always mean they are best, and a lesser-known brand may end up being the more appropriate one for your equipment. Some extra research on your part about media compatibility for your recorder may save you money and headaches.

III

Third, with any magnetic tape medium—whether the signal is analog or digital—microscopic layers of the metallic coating that carry the signal wear off each time it is played. With analog formats this wear results in a gradual increase of noise and decrease in signal strength. "Tape hiss" becomes prominent, and copying reproduces (and sometimes emphasizes) that hiss. "Generation loss" refers to the incremental loss in quality that results from making copies of analog recordings (and copies of those copies). Noise reduction systems such as Dolby can be used to suppress, but not eliminate, hiss.

Digital recordings do not suffer from such a gradual weakening of signal strength. Instead, you might encounter a sudden loss of all information from a portion of a recording. This may be manifested by short bursts of noise called "drop outs" or, in worse case scenarios, by a tape that is completely unplayable. In either case—digital or analog—it is a good idea to make backup copies of your field recordings as soon as possible and avoid playing the originals. Refreshing backups every few years is a good practice as well.

Finally, analog recordings made on magnetic tape are susceptible to a phenomenon called "print through." A strong magnetic signal may slightly remagnetize the signal on the next layer of tape. The result is a kind of delay and echo effect that can ruin a recording. "Print through" typically occurs when the tape is rewound before storage; this packs the layers of tape tightly, and the thinner the tape, the greater the danger. Good storage practice can largely avoid this problem—use the play function, and not rewind or fast-forward, to bring the tape to an end before storage.

Equipment and accessories

The following section serves as a guide to different kinds of recording equipment, media, and accessories for audio, video, and photographic field research. We have listed the advantages and disadvantages of some of the most frequently encountered recording formats as of July 2001.

Audio equipment

1.Reel-to-reel tape (also called "open-reel")

In open-reel tape systems, the tape is threaded manually to wind off a source reel, past the recording and playback heads, and onto a separate take-up reel. Open-reel tape appeared in the mid-1940s, and is still considered an excellent recording medium and a standard archival format. Common recording speeds for open-reel recorders are 7 1/2, 3 3/4, and 1 7/8 ips (inches per second), although 15 or 30 ips is considered the "professional standard." Higher speed equals higher recording quality.

Advantages:
- Recorder models being manufactured today (e.g. Nagra, Uher, Tascam, Studer) produce professional-quality recordings
- Film synchronization capability
- Media is easy to splice, either in the event of breakage or for editing
- Media is archival standard, with proven life of fifty years ("preservation quality")
- Very long recording times are possible

Disadvantages:
- Equipment is heavy and may be difficult to operate; media is bulky
- Consumer-grade equipment is no longer manufactured and playback facilities are increasingly limited
- Professional equipment is expensive
- Maintenance requirements may be considerable and finding capable repairpersons is difficult

2. Audiocassette

Philips introduced the audiocassette in 1963, intending it for dictation. The format proved so popular that tape formulations were gradually improved to permit higher-fidelity results. However, the precision of this format is limited mainly by the fact that key parts of the guiding mechanism are located inside each removable cassette, introducing variation from one playing to the next.

Advantages:
- Inexpensive recording/playback equipment is widely available
- Compact size of equipment and tape makes for easy carrying and unobtrusive recording
- Easy to operate
- High-quality, durable equipment available; good track record as a field medium
- Proven archival lifespan: 25-year-old audiotapes are still playable
- Less susceptible to dust and mishandling than open-reel tape

Disadvantages:
- No cassette tape is considered to be "preservation quality"
- Recording speed varies, although standard speed is supposed to be 1 7/8 inches per second
- Sound quality is inferior to reel-to-reel or digital recorders
- Tape 1 mm thick or less (found in 120 or 100 minute cassettes) is particularly prone to breakage and print-through
- Cassettes are typically limited to no more than 50 minutes per side

Note: "Bias" refers to a high frequency signal generated by a recording device and mixed with the external input signal. This high frequency signal is designed to reduce distortion by normalizing the tape's response to audio input.

III

There are three standard levels of bias for audiotape: Type I (low bias), Type II (high bias), and Type IV (metal). Type I generally has a "thin" sound and more "hiss." On the other hand, Type IV tape is usually compatible only with the latest, most sophisticated recorders.

Many tape recorders have a bias setting that should be adjusted to match the kind of tape being used. Some analog tape recorders are adjusted for bias at the factory to work best with one specific kind of audiotape, and this is often identified in the documentation. There is no one kind of tape that is best with all recorders, either open-reel or audiocassette. Research and experimentation are the best routes to producing quality recordings.

3. Microcassette

First introduced by Olympus in 1969, the "microcassette" is a scaled-down audiocassette designed for voice recording. It is still used in hand-held dictation machines and telephone answering machines.

Advantages:
- Wide variety of inexpensive recorders available
- Equipment is compact and portable
- Easy to operate
- Can record up to three hours on a very small tape

Disadvantages:
- Poorest sound quality of all formats listed, with standard tape speeds of 15/16 or 15/32 inches per second
- Very limited dynamic range aimed at achieving intelligible voice recording only; unsuitable for other types of recording

• Usually offers no provision for signal output
   to transfer recordings to other media

4. DAT (Digital Audio Tape)

DAT arose in the mid-1980s to accommodate
digitally recorded and reproduced music. Due to the
encoding technology, it can handle the massive
amounts of digital data required for sound recording.
It has quickly become an industry standard, although
not without drawbacks and competition. DAT stock
comes in either data grade or music grade; data grade
are generally cheaper and work perfectly for
recording sound. See *www.solorb.com/dat-heads/* for
current and archived information on the DAT format.

III

Advantages:
   • High quality digital sound signal (24 bit; 44.1k
      or 48k sampling rates)
   • Compact size of recorder and tape
   • Ease of operation
   • Make exact copies without "generation loss"
   • Absolute time-code reference written to tapes
      during recording
Disadvantages:
   • Some tape can exhibit high dropout rate
   • Equipment may be particularly sensitive
      to dampness and dust
   • Not yet time-tested as an archival or field
      medium
   • Relatively expensive

5. MiniDisc

MiniDiscs were announced in 1991 by Sony as a disc-based digital medium for recording and distributing consumer audio. MiniDisc uses a compression algorithm to store large amounts of audio data, which is why it is referred to as "near CD quality." Current debates surround the questions of compression and loss of audio quality (see Schüller 1999); some feel the compression lends a more "natural" quality to the digital sound, while others fear that too much original audio signal is lost. The disc is enclosed in a small (7cm x 7cm), convenient, cartridge. See *www.minidisc.org* for more information on the technology and history of MiniDisc.

Advantages:
- Very compact size of recorder and discs
- Relatively inexpensive
- Ease of operation
- Benefit of digital sound

Disadvantages:
- Compressed audio data
- Not yet time-tested as a field or storage medium
- Equipment may be sensitive to dampness and dust
- Digital signal must be converted to analog in order to copy, whether copies are analog or digital

Film/Video Equipment

Motion picture film consists of a flexible transparent film (acetate or polyester) containing a sequence of still images advanced by perforations along the side, with each image exposed for a fraction of a second before a projection lamp to create the illusion of motion. A good general FAQ is found at *http://www.redballoon.net/~snorwood/faq2.html*.

1. 16mm film with analog or digital sound

Introduced in 1923 for home-movies, but it has found a number of uses including lower-budget feature films and documentaries.

Advantages:
- Long considered the highest quality medium for visual documentation (short of 35mm film used in theaters)
- Proven archival life

Disadvantages:
- Expensive and complex medium to master and duplicate
- Equipment, film stock, and developing are expensive
- Cumbersome operation; assistance of second person usually necessary
- More distortion than digital video, although viewers are often used to the types of distortion introduced by film (and do not notice them)

2. 8mm film

Introduced in 1932, 8mm motion picture film was

intended for use by amateurs and home-movie aficionados. In 1965, an improved 8mm film format called Super-8 was introduced with smaller perforations and a resultant larger image area.

Advantages:
- Compact and inexpensive relative to 16mm equipment

Disadvantages:
- Format no longer in general use
- Lower resolution than 16mm film
- Recording and playback equipment difficult to find: although Super-8 film stock is still manufactured, standard 8mm film stock is no longer available
- Transfer to video can be expensive if done with specialized equipment on a frame-by-frame basis (alternatively, a film can be projected and the resulting picture can be videotaped without much distortion)

3. Videocassette

The following is a list of video formats that you may encounter, either in the field or during archiving/ editing. The list is not exhaustive, but rather provides basic advantages and disadvantages for each format. To get more extensive information, read trade magazines, use the World Wide Web, and continue to keep up with ongoing discussions and debates!

For a basic primer on different widely-available formats used in consumer and broadcast situations, look at *www.cybercollege.com/tvp047.htm*.

Betacam SP (see: *betacam.palsite.com/format.html*)

Developed by Sony in the mid-1980s, and still the predominant format for field acquisition and post-production in the broadcast world. Betacam uses cassettes and transports similar to the Betamax home video format, but the similarity ends there. Tape speed is higher, and color reproduction is more accurate. Betamax is the consumer version of the format introduced in 1976 but it is not found very often anymore.

Advantages:
- Professional quality
- Relatively easy to use

Disadvantages:
- Very expensive
- Heavy and bulky equipment
- Short running time of tape (45 to 60 minutes)
- Equipment is often professional level, requiring some expertise to use

3/4" (U-Matic)

Another Sony format, with three different versions: LB, HB and SP. U-Matic LB (Low Band) has been around from the early 1970s and is one of the oldest cassette video formats. HB (High Band) has increased color resolution, while SP has both increased color and light reproducing capabilities.

U-Matic is commonly known as "3/4 inch", referring to tape width. Although it is still a popular production format alternative to Betacam SP, you are unlikely to encounter 3/4" as a field recording medium today. However, LB and HB U-Matic tapes are often used for archiving because of the relatively low tape costs and low recording density, which makes the tapes robust against aging.

Advantages:
- Standard industrial video format
- Production (broadcast) quality

Disadvantages:
- Expensive
- Weight and bulk of equipment
- Bulk of tape
- Less commonly used today

1/2" (VHS; camcorder)

Consumer format introduced in late 1970s (competed with Betamax and won); probably the most popular format in terms of viewing copies. But while 1/2" playback decks are found all over the world, VHS cameras are increasingly rare.

Advantages:
- Easy to use
- Widely available

Disadvantages:
- Not production quality
- Generally poor audio quality
- Bulky and heavy camcorders

Super VHS

Introduced in early 1980s as an improvement over VHS; technically higher quality, and used by some broadcast companies to record in the field.

Advantages:
- Much higher resolution than VHS (about 400 lines versus 230 for regular VHS)
- Production quality

Disadvantages:
- Requires special high-quality video cassettes and playback equipment

8mm video

Introduced in the 1980s to replace Betamax in the consumer market. Reduced size of the tape cassette meant that cameras could be made even smaller than VHS camcorders—a definite benefit for field recording. The quality of 8mm video is similar to VHS though, which means that it has not been used as a professional format.

Advantages:
- Digital audio available
- Portable and compact
- Easy to use

Disadvantages:
- Not considered production quality (better than VHS though, with 270 lines of resolution)
- Some models have no means of overriding auto recording level
- Will soon be replaced in consumer market by digital video

Hi8

At about the time that S-VHS appeared, Sony came out with Hi8, a higher quality version of 8mm. Hi8 can be used as an acquisition (field recording) format by broadcasters, and under optimum conditions can produce high quality video.

Advantages:
- Much higher resolution than 8mm (about 400 lines)
- Digital audio available
- Portable and compact
- Easy to use
- Recording times of up to two hours

Disadvantages:
- Requires special video cassettes and playback equipment
- Thin tape; does not stand up well to repeated playing
- Notoriously high dropout rate
- Will soon be replaced in consumer market by digital video

Digital Video

Multiple video formats have entered the digital arena, and are fast becoming professional and consumer-level standards. Below is a brief list of some of the different types of digital video formats.

Digital Betacam

Digital successor to the Betacam SP format. Introduced by Sony in 1993, it uses physically similar half-inch cassettes and is a professional (i.e. expensive) format.

DV/DVCAM/DVCPRO (see *www.dvcentral.org/ dvwhat.html*)

DV (formerly DVC) is a format backed by manufacturers such as Sony, Philips, Canon, Thomson, Hitachi, and Panasonic. It was the first digital recording format within reach of consumer-level markets. DV uses a 5:1 ratio to compress image data, but despite this compression the picture quality is usually better than Hi8. MiniDV is the compact version of DV, designed for use in consumer and prosumer level camcorders. DVCPRO is Panasonic's professional variant of the DV standard. The major difference is doubled tape speed in DVCPRO, which results in better dropout tolerance and general recording robustness. DVCAM is Sony's variation, sitting somewhere between miniDV and DVCPRO. MiniDV cameras are going to be affordable for amateurs and professionals while DVCAM cameras are much more expensive. Because miniDV produces excellent quality images, however, the upper-end miniDV cameras have features associated with professional cameras like interchangeable lenses and manual control of audio inputs.

Advantages:
- High resolution of image (about 540 lines)
- Ease of use
- High sound quality (48K, 16 bit, stereo)
- Portable and compact
- Easy to bring into digital editing system

Disadvantages:
- Expensive (though prices are falling)
- Low archival life of miniDV tapes (some

III

estimate only 10 years; DVCAM is more stable)
- Not extensively field-tested
- Relatively short tape length (60 min for miniDV, 184 minutes for DVCAM)
- Video signal is compressed (though high quality)
- MiniDV can be prone to image "dropouts" (though not as much as Hi8)

Microphones

Microphones are a crucial part of the recording system. They come in a variety of shapes and sizes and range in cost from less than $100 to over $1,000. It is worth buying the best you can afford, but first educate yourself about microphones that are compatible with your recorder, appropriate microphones for your recording situation (indoor/outdoor; individual/group), and effective microphone placement (for more information on microphones see Jackson, chapter 11, and entries in White's *The Audio Dictionary*). You may need to take more than one type of microphone into the field. Even if you have a very expensive recording deck your recording will suffer with a cheaper mic. The mic is the first device in your recording chain, and your recording cannot be better than the signal your mic is capable of reproducing.

To record stereo sound, you will need either two microphones or one "single-point" stereo microphone—the latter are less flexible but quick and easy to set up. Some recording equipment does not allow you the choice; if you can choose, consider your anticipated recording environment before deciding.

Types of transducers

There are two common types in use, the dynamic and the condenser. The dynamic mic has a diaphragm that moves in response to air pressure and generates a small amount of electricity patterned to the pressure waves. Dynamic mics are capable of handling more physical and sonic abuse and are typically used to mic instruments and vocals up close. Many have a frequency curve that is specialized for a particular instrument. Condenser mics use a lighter diaphragm and require a power supply. The distinction "electret condenser" means that the mic uses a battery power supply or phantom power (power supplied by the recording device or mixer) while a regular condenser uses phantom power .

1. Dynamic

Advantages:
- Extremely rugged
- Can tolerate extreme temperature and humidity
- Very good sound quality possible
- Affordable
- No batteries or phantom power needed to operate
- Can tolerate very loud sounds (without damage)

Disadvantages:
- Mic models are usually tailored to be sensitive to particular frequency ranges
- Lower electrical signal output may raise noise floor
- Need to be very close to sound source for optimal results

2. Condenser (also known as capacitor or electret condenser)

Advantages:
- Excellent sound quality—very clean and crisp
- Wide, flat frequency response
- Can be very small in size (e.g. lavalier)
- High electrical signal output with good signal-to-noise ratio
- Sensitive to low level sound

Disadvantages:
- Needs some form of power to operate
- Very fragile physical design
- Range from expensive to very expensive
- Loud sounds can overpower or damage the mic

Directionality

Directionality refers to the spatial pattern with which a microphone responds to sound. The following are the major types of microphones commonly used in ethnomusicological research:

Omnidirectional

This pattern picks up sounds in a 360-degree spatial pattern, though not necessarily equally.

Advantages:
- Good for group interviews or large groups such as choirs if placed properly

Disadvantages:
- Picks up background noise from all directions
- Needs to be used relatively close to source

Directional (unidirectional)

This pattern rejects sounds coming from behind while accepting those coming from in front of the microphone. An extreme directional mic is called a shotgun mic. These are very effective at focusing on certain sound sources when one must be 10 feet away or farther.

Advantages:
- Can be used farther away than omnidirectional microphones
- Unwanted background sounds are not picked up as readily

Disadvantages:
- Can only be effectively used for sound from a single source (doesn't pick up widely spaced performers well)
- Placement with shotgun mics must be carefully controlled and monitored for good sound
- Shotgun mics can be long and obtrusive; in the wrong context they can be mistaken for a gun barrel

Cardioid (directional)

One of the most common directionally-specific formats, it records in a frontal direction using a heart-shaped pattern. This means it picks up front and side sounds, with a small amount of rear sounds. There is a range of cardioid patterns; some can be adjusted.

Advantages:
- Reduces reverberation, ambience, and background noises
- Often used for musical applications to isolate sound source
- Records both sonic source (strongly) as well as ambient sound (weakly), which is desired in some situations

Disadvantages:
- Microphone placement is crucial—may reject too much reverberation or create a dead spot

Hypercardioid
With this pattern, directionality is based on the cardioid pattern, but the effect is more pronounced.

Figure-eight pattern
This mic format responds to sounds at the front and back but not on sides, or may be placed so that it responds to sounds from the sides. When used the second way, in combination with a cardioid microphone oriented toward the sound source, the technique is called "M-S (mid-side) stereo pair microphone technique."

Advantages:
- When using the M-S technique, deadspots are virtually eliminated
- The stereo image can be changed without moving microphone

Disadvantages:
 • A matrix or special stereo setup is needed to
   properly record or play back the audio image

Stereo mics

These have two separate mics within a single
housing ("single-point"). You usually can't adjust the
kind of stereo image you get but they are very
convenient to work with. Be aware of the kind of
connections needed. Some stereo mics output to a
modified XLR connector that is not a true balanced
signal. This type of connector must usually be adapted
to a stereo miniplug or dual 1/4" jacks. This is fine as
long as you do not use more than a few feet of
microphone cable. Others have a 5-pin output that then
connects to two true balanced outputs. This allows you
to use very long cable lengths without picking up hum.

Advantages
 • Compact method for stereo recording
 • Easy to setup and move
 • Relatively cheap, compared to stereo pair mics
Disadvantages
 • Limited control over depth of stereo image
 • Not as versatile in terms of placement

Physical design

There are various microphone designs. Each has a more or less specific recording application; be sure your mic can handle the situations you will be in.

Handheld

These can also be mounted on stand, and are the most commonly seen and versatile design. They can be used for music recording, as well as for interviews.

Lavalier ("lapel" or "tie-tack)

Small and unobtrusive, this design is good for interviews. The microphone elements are very small and fragile; lavalier mics do not work well for music.

Surface-mount (PZM)

These can be used on a table for interviews, but are often used on stages for live musical and theatrical recordings.

Shotgun

A unidirectional mic that only accepts sound within a small angle. These are useful when you need to exclude a majority of ambient sound, such as when the sound source is quite distant from the mic. They are not good for music and not very effective in a crowded room if the source is more than 20 feet away.

Wireless

Freedom from cables, but these can suffer from signal interference. Only use mics that come in the 160–171 MHz range; 49MHz wireless mics should be avoided. Sound quality will not be as good as a mic with cables, and good systems are expensive.

Electrical impedance

Electrical impedance is a characteristic of equipment that is expressed in ohms. If high and low impedance equipment is used together, a matching transformer will be required.

Low impedance, or low Z, is 600 ohms or less. Advantage is that low Z microphones allow the use of very long cable runs (up to 1,000 feet) with little loss of sound quality.

High impedance, or high Z, is 10,000 ohms or higher. High Z microphones begin to sound muffled after 20 feet of cable. Also, they are prone to interference from fluorescent lights and other sources. High Z signals are usually associated with electric instruments (e.g. guitars) and PA systems.

Audio cables ordinarily act like antennas, picking up magnetic interference from the air or from the current running through the very same wire. The longer the cable, the more hum and noise it will pick up. A balanced signal uses two wires to carry the same signal and then a third only carries a ground signal. These cables typically have 3-pin XLR connectors. The identical signals are sent out of phase and then compared at the destination to cancel out the noise the cable has picked up.

Microphone Accessories

Windscreens

If you will be recording outdoors, invest in a good windscreen. The foam rubber screens that sometimes come with microphones are generally not effective.

Instead, purchase a good quality "fur"-type windscreen. This can practically eliminate wind noise on your recordings.

Stands

Investing in a mic stand can improve the quality of your recordings. Different types of stands exist, including tabletop, boom, and lightweight (with folding legs). Choose the one that best fits your needs, keeping packability in mind if you will be traveling a lot with your equipment. Also be aware that a small tripod can double as a microphone stand with the right adapters.

Shock Mounts

If you will be mounting your microphone on a video camera or even a stationary stand, it is a good idea to purchase a shock mount. These mounts suspend the microphone, often with a system of shock cord or other elastic material, helping to reduce vibration noise caused by movement (of the microphone itself or of people/things near the microphone).

Photographic equipment

There are several types of still cameras that are available for use in fieldwork. Some are easier to use than others. As with recording media, choose the equipment that is most appropriate for your project and your budget, and become familiar with operation and maintenance of your equipment before taking it to the field.

1. 35mm single-lens reflex (SLR)

Advantages:
- Most versatile type of 35mm camera
- Through-the-lens light meter
- Exposure, focus, shutter speed and f-stop number are viewed through the lens
- A range of lenses can be used
- Good cameras can be used in fully manual or automatic modes

Disadvantages:
- Electronically and mechanically complex, increasing the potential for malfunction
- Shutter can be noisy
- Can be difficult to focus in low light
- Many new models rely heavily on batteries

2. 2" single-lens reflex

Advantages:
- Produces a sharp negative
- Good for copy work
- Quiet

Disadvantages:
- Expensive
- Bulky

3. Twin-lens reflex (TLR)

Advantages:
- Mechanically simple
- Easy to use
- Quiet shutter
- Large negative (2 1/4"x 2 1/4")

Disadvantages:
- Bulky and heavy
- No built-in light meter
- Lenses are not interchangeable on all models
- You don't see exactly what the lens sees

4. Rangefinder camera (35mm and larger negative sizes)

Advantages:
- Easy to use
- Through-the-lens light meter
- Light and compact
- Quiet

Disadvantages:
- You don't see exactly what the lens sees
- Images small and therefore difficult to focus
- Generally lenses are not interchangeable

5. Compact autofocusing camera ("point and shoot")

Advantages:
- Easy to use; functions are usually fully automatic
- Small and lightweight
- Built-in flash
- 35mm format is common worldwide

Disadvantages:
- You cannot check depth of field
- Lenses are not interchangeable
- Complete reliance on battery power (for most)
- Many models do not allow override of automatic controls

6. Digital still cameras

Digital technology is rapidly changing still photography, and new technology appears with increasing frequency. To familiarize yourself with some basic options and terms, see the digital camera FAQ at *www.dcresource.com/faq/faq.html*.

Advantages:
- Does not require film development or developing costs
- Liquid crystal display (LCD) allows the photographer to see the captured image immediately after it is taken

- Does not require scanning for use in digitized presentations
- Very quiet operation; no shutter click or film advance noise

Disadvantages:
- Lower resolution than film: the very best digital cameras have a resolution of about 2000 pixels per inch (usually much lower) compared to the equivalent of about 10,000 pixels per inch for film
- Less grayscale depth than film; 12-bit digital provides only 4096 shades
- Tend to be more expensive and complicated to fix than conventional cameras
- Heavily dependant on batteries

III

Other Essential Equipment

1. Power supply

Find out what your "power environment" will be; adapters/converters are available for use with some equipment and may be necessary in parts of the world that use different voltages and currents. While portable recording systems (video or audio) come with the option of AC (wall plug) or DC (battery power), there are also aftermarket power options available. Many field recording situations will require you to use battery power, and many recording units have notoriously unreliable internal battery packs. Do your homework on this before purchasing or borrowing a piece of equipment to take into the field! A good external battery pack may end up being a worthwhile investment.

In addition to external batteries, you can also purchase extra on-board batteries for equipment like video cameras and DAT machines. This is a good idea, as many of the rechargeable batteries supplied with such equipment eventually build up what is called "memory." This means that a battery (usually a Nickel Cadmium or NiCad) has gone through multiple cycles of recharge without complete discharge, and has effectively lost capacity. That is, at one point it could hold 100% charge, and now may only be able to hold 80% even though the charger indicates the battery is completely charged. Lead acid batteries do not form memory, and these are used in most external battery packs. They also can power equipment for as much as 10 hours. However, they are heavy and slow to charge. Lithium Ion batteries were designed to increase battery life and combat memory issues. These are starting to appear in external battery packs, but they are a bit more expensive. For more information on power options, check out these two web sites: *www.ecocharge.com* and *www.bescor.com/*.

2. Tripods

Tripods are useful for still photography and essential for good videography or film recording. They can also serve as microphone stands with the use of thread adapters. Many tripod makes and models exist, but consider these issues:

- Inexpensive tripods are rarely very stable. Some have the advantage of being lightweight, but may only be practical for still photography using very light cameras.

- Video and film work requires a tripod that will remain steady and is tall enough *with only the legs* extended to reach eye level. Despite the fact that even high-end tripods include an extendable centerpost, its use should be avoided because these are susceptible to vibration.

- Smooth pans in video and film require a good quality fluid (or video) head. On high quality tripods, the head is purchased separately from the tripod legs and is tailored to the specific videographic or photographic needs of the user.

• Consider the use of a monopod in crowded places where a tripod is impractical or dangerous. While it does not offer the same stability as a tripod, a monopod can eliminate much of the vertical movement of a handheld camera.

3. Adapters

You need to anticipate a variety of recording situations and be prepared. For example, the people you will be working with may make their own recordings, use amplifiers and mixers, or have extensive audio libraries of their own. Besides having all the adapters you need to run equipment on its own, you may want to be able to plug into a sound system or another tape recorder. If you intend to leave copies of recordings in the source community, you need to know local standards and equipment.

4. Accessories

For audio and video recordings there are accessories available for cleaning, making connections, viewing, or listening to recordings. These include such things as cleaning cassettes, RCA cables/adapters, portable video monitors, and headphones. Be sure to collect all potentially necessary accessories before heading to the field.

IV.
Success with Your Equipment:
Procedures for Recording in the Field

As you develop strategies for your research before, during, and after fieldwork, consider the same factors you weighed in the process of choosing equipment—the nature of your research, field conditions, and the intended use of the materials. This section should help you formulate procedures for each phase of your work.

Before You Leave for the Field

IV

Training and dress rehearsal

Explore local resources for learning to operate any new equipment that you will use in the field. Proper training in equipment setup and use will save time and avoid distress during field research. Workshops on field recording technology will be important in increasing your expertise, but they can also be great ways to get hands-on experience with equipment comparable to that which you may buy for yourself. These may offer the opportunity for you to learn any routine or emergency maintenance procedures that recording devices could require. Becoming familiar with simple repairs and cleaning techniques is always a good idea for any piece of equipment that you will use.

Set up and practice recording before leaving for the field. Make sure all your equipment works: try external and battery powering, use all of the recording options, and experiment with microphones and microphone placement. Correct problems that arise and try again until you get results that you are satisfied with. Today's sophisticated electronic equipment will most likely manifest any manufacturing defects within the first thirty days. Make sure you procure your equipment well before you leave in the event that you need to replace or return it.

Any documentary equipment is going to require a certain amount of technical knowledge as well as some operating skill. Good photography is not just about learning "f-stops" and shutter speeds, but also depends on effective composition. Microphone placement can have a tremendous impact on the quality of an audio recording. These are aesthetic dimensions to be sure, and realizing your vision will take practice. If you plan to do still photography, take many pictures before you leave and evaluate the results critically. Have someone else with some skill and experience in the medium evaluate them as well. Making good audio and visual recordings is no different than learning to play a musical instrument—it takes practice and investing in the effort up front will help you in the field when it is time to "perform."

IV

Backup equipment

Do enough documentary work and you will eventually experience equipment failure, loss, or theft. As careful as you may be about maintenance and security, you can count on something going wrong, especially with more mechanically and electronically complex devices (e.g. DAT machines). When investing so much in equipment, it is easy to forget about having some kind of backup. Reserve equipment is especially important when working in isolated or extreme environmental conditions such as a desert or tropical rainforest. A $50 handheld tape recorder may be a lifesaver when an $1800 DAT deck fails midway through the field research on a $30,000 fellowship.

Develop a checklist

Before leaving for the field, make sure that you have everything you need. A checklist will help you organize and evaluate your equipment. Below are some common items to consider.

IV

1. Recording equipment (audio and/or video)

___microphones/stands/windscreens/microphone
     cables
___cables and adapters
___mixer
___headphones
___batteries
___tape/storage containers for tape
___head cleaner and demagnetizer

2. Still camera and accessories (lenses, filters, etc.)

___batteries
___flash equipment
___film/storage containers
___lens-cleaning accessories: dust brush, lens
      cloth, cleaning fluid
___carrying case
___tripod

3. Computer (power supply and accessories)

___software
___carrying case
___printer, case, extra cartridge, and paper
___extra disks/storage containers
___extra batteries, A/C adapter, voltage adapter

IV

4. Supplies

___notepads
___pens, pencils and waterproof marking pens
___calculator (and batteries)
___flashlight (and batteries)
___penknife
___duct tape (to fasten cables)

In the Field

If you are recording alone, as many fieldworkers do, you will have many tasks to take care of simultaneously. Even if you do have help, organization of tasks is key. Good preparation will make the experience less stressful and help you produce better results.

Permission

Permission to make and use recordings should ideally be obtained in writing. An alternative is to record a performer or person to be interviewed verbally giving you permission to make the recording. Bring your permission forms and have participants fill them out before recording, or record them verbally at the beginning of the tape.

Equipment setup

Where you put your equipment and microphone may be constrained by your permission agreement, etiquette and/or musical layout. There are too many variables to give you adequate guidelines here, but keep these two principles in mind:

- Get your mics as close as possible to your desired sources, and
- Arriving early gives you an advantage. You have time to carefully set up, to scope out the best places for mics, secure cords, and generally prepare.

Operating recording equipment

Check and monitor input levels on audio equipment. Make sure that the input signal does not "peak" or distort; some equipment will have a peak indicator (often a red LED) that lights up when an input signal exceeds 0 dbv (the optimal sound level). Important note: VU meters do not indicate very short intense peaks (such as a gunshot or a drum strike) and this is why there are separate peak meters. VU meters do not respond quickly enough and so without a peak meter, you could be experiencing preamp clipping without knowing it. Occasional peaks in sound levels are not a problem (and are often unavoidable), but a performance or interview recorded well over 0 dbv will be distorted and possibly unusable.

Include important announcements at the beginning of each tape/segment. Make an audio or video recording announcing pertinent information (imagine the label falling off of a tape); also record verbal permission to record in lieu of or in addition to a written agreement. An A440 pitch recorded at the start of each tape will ensure that it can be played back at the proper speed.

IV

Media

Prevent accidental rerecording over your tapes or discs by "locking" or "write-protecting" them. With audiocassettes and some videocassettes, this is done by breaking out a plastic tab, but with DATs, MiniDisc, 8mm video, and DV, this is done by sliding a tab to the "locked" position.

Tape numbering and labeling

Choose a simple numbering system such as consecutive numbers or the year of fieldwork followed by the number (e.g., 92–25).

Tapes should be linked to all relevant documentation by use of the same number (See Chapter 1).

After a recording session

Once you have finished a recording, there is still much to do. Use the following brief list as a guideline.

Equipment care
- Make sure switches are off
- Put equipment back in cases; wind cords; remove and recharge batteries
- Develop a regular maintenance plan for equipment (cleaning and demagnetizing tape heads, etc.)

Dubbing/Media
- Immediately spot check recordings for equipment malfunctions or operator error
- Write up your documentation on the recording process for that session
- Prepare backup tapes in the field if you have access to dubbing equipment
- Make copies for informants (if you have agreed to provide them)
- Send duplicate set home before you leave the field; if you have visitors, send duplicates home with them when they go
- Never edit original tapes unless it is part of your permission agreements

Storage
- Check your equipment before taking it to the next setup
- Store properly, especially for extended periods between recording sessions

IV

V.
Storing and Preserving
Your Materials

Storing Your Materials

Planning for fieldwork includes considering how your data will be stored, both in the field and at home. Materials and equipment that are improperly cared for in the field may not be usable by the researcher at home. Months, or years, of collecting can be obliterated by careless handling of the recording media. If the data is worth collecting and using in research, its physical condition over time should be carefully monitored.

When you do fieldwork, you generate data in a variety of formats (magnetic tape, film, paper, computer disk), all of which should be preserved if you intend to reuse material at a later date or to make it available to researchers in future generations.

Storing research data is probably the most cumbersome and confusing task for fieldworkers in any discipline. Concern for climate, safety, and data organization can easily be put aside when other matters relating to research are present. Yet they remain of extreme importance throughout the research period, in the field, and at home. Unfortunately, the issues relating to storage continue to grow and get more complex as recording formats

V

change, become obsolete, and are superseded.

Deterioration of fieldwork data, including field tapes, film, photographs, papers, and computer disks, can result from a number of factors. These include acidity, fungus, mold, pollution, temperature, humidity, light, insects, rodents, poor handling, and disasters. It is essential that you protect your data.

In the field the greatest threats come from temperature (usually heat but also dramatic changes in temperature), humidity, and excessive handling. Heat causes magnetic tape to curl and to become brittle; it causes paper to deteriorate more quickly. High humidity can cause mildew and other fungi to develop. Repeated use of tapes and overhandling photographs and papers speeds up their deterioration considerably. Try to keep your media in a dry, dust-free environment with a stable temperature. The single most important precaution to take is to prevent large changes in temperature and dampness from affecting your recording media and equipment. A picnic cooler with a desiccant is often sufficient for the short term.

Refer to the 1985 publication *Preserving Field Records* (Kensworthy, King, Ruwell, and Van Houton) for detailed recommendations on optimal preservation conditions for paper, film, tape, and machine-readable records. Included is a timeline for preserving field data compiled by Eleanor M. King. Most of the following recommendations are included in her chapter on film, tape, and video.

V

1. Sound and Video Recordings

- Always use high quality tape
- Do not use extra-long tapes (in any format), as they are thinner and prone to problems
- Always make copies of originals for working use; Originals should then be stored in a safe place
- Store tapes in their boxes to keep out dirt and dust
- All tapes should be stored vertically, in a dust-free and fireproof environment
- Keep all recorded media at least two feet from electrical fixtures and power lines and away from magnetic fields in speakers and amplifiers
- The ideal temperature for tape storage is 62°–68° F (17°–20°C), and the relative humidity should be between 30 and 40 percent
- Tapes should always be kept out of attics, basements, or porches where extreme temperatures will damage them; they should also be kept away from radiators and woodstoves and out of the direct sunlight
- Recording and playback equipment should be cleaned and demagnetized regularly
- Tapes should be stored tails out and wound at play speed for long-term storage
- Label and number all tapes

V

2. Film

- Use low speed (ASA/ISO number), fine- grain film whenever possible
- Use black and white as well as color film for documentation; black and white film has greater archival longevity
- Store film and equipment in the field in as cool and dry a place as possible; do not store film or equipment in car trunks or glove compartments; relative humidity should be between 30 and 45 per cent
- Choose processing laboratories that provide archival-quality procedures, including extra washing to remove all destabilizing chemicals
- Have duplicate copies of all photographic media prepared, and store them in a safe place
- Use acid-free papers and encasing products that do not contain PVC for storing master prints, slides, and negatives
- Keep a log of all your photographs, especially masters and originals; label all negatives, slides, and prints to correspond with the log
- Write on the backs of prints or on slide mounts with a soft lead pencil only
- Store original motion picture film reels in a cool environment; keep the reels flat to prevent the film from sagging
- Inspect visual media regularly to catch deterioration before it becomes irreparable

V

3. Paper

(Recommendations by Trudy Van Houton from
her article on preserving paper records in
Preserving Field Records)

- Use acid-free paper for all field documents.
  When acidic paper is used, make a permanent
  copy by photocopying it onto acid-free paper
- Legibility and careful labeling of papers is
  extremely important
- Keep field records in acid free folders and
  in boxes to protect them from harmful
  ultraviolet (UV) light
- Paper records should be kept cool and
  protected from wide fluctuations in
  temperature; the humidity level should be
  between 40 and 60 per cent
- Protect paper records from insects and rodents
  by keeping them in metal boxes
- Use carbon printer ribbons and pencils for
  writing—these are the safest writing media;
  photocopy any documents that use felt tip
  or ballpoint pens
- Do not use steel paperclips or staples—they
  tend to rust and destroy the edges of the
  paper records to which they are attached;
  instead, use plastic clips or stainless steel
  or aluminum staples

4. Computer-generated records
(based on recommendations by Trudy Van Houton in *Preserving Field Records*)

- Keep up with current technology by converting all files to up-to-date formats
- Disks should be stored upright at a steady temperature, between 50° and 120° F; the humidity level should be between 40 and 70 per cent
- Copy disks every two to three years
- Do not expose disks to magnetic fields from nearby televisions, telephones, electrical equipment, monitors, or disk drives
- Make backup copies for all files
- Write-protect disks unless they are being updated
- Label all disks and keep a record of files (and the programs used) on each disk
- Keep documentation for gaining access to all files
- Provide hard copy printouts of all files

Depositing Fieldwork Materials in Archives

When your fieldwork and research is completed, you will be left with quantities of data on audio and/or videotapes, photographs, field notes, and computer disks. Careful thought should be given to the decision about what to do with this material. Although you may elect to store materials in your home or office, you might wish to consider the long term advantages of institutional deposit. An institutional archive is more likely to have better climate control capabilities and generally offers greater protection against loss by fire or theft. Some archives provide gratis collector's copies for depositors (i.e., making a second "working copy" available to the collector) while protecting the originals.

Many researchers today make recordings with the view to publish them either traditionally on CD or on the Web. With this in mind they feel they need to keep hold of the originals. These people might consider the following:

- Publishing is important but it does not preserve the originals
- Normally only "highlights" from collections are selected for publication. There may be items of great musical interest that are not of sufficiently high technical quality to publish. Complete collections and complete recordings can be preserved and made accessible via an archival institution.

Archival repositories for fieldwork data are found in various locations throughout the world and have diverse scopes and missions. Some local historical societies, libraries, archives, or museums house archival collections, especially oral history materials. Regional centers welcome documentation of local traditions, while national and international institutions provide a broader research base, housing materials that represent cultures from around the world.

When selecting an institution, it is important to consider:

- The availability of proper storage conditions
- Provision for restricted public access, if desired
- The ability to provide prompt and accurate bibliographic description (cataloging) as well as copies of the original materials
- The general scope and mission of the institution (can it cope with multimedia collections, for example, or will your collection need to be split between institutions?)
- Whether the institution is financially secure (is its funding likely to run out?)

You may wish to deposit in two archives, one accessible to local scholars and community members, the other easily available to your colleagues. Wherever you decide to deposit your collections, make sure you notify artists/musicians/informants who may have an interest in the material. This may be a good opportunity to also consult informants about sensitive material—there may be items they consider inappropriate to deposit in certain institutions.

Storage

Archives make every effort to preserve and store fieldwork materials so that they will be available to future generations of researchers. Archivists are interested in conservation, especially of original documents. If you are concerned about the storage and care of your fieldwork data, you should check with the institution to find out what its policies and practices are for document preservation and request a tour of the facility. Here are a few basic principles to keep in mind:

- Storage areas should have reliable temperature and humidity control and be free of dirt, dust, insects, and rodents
- Field tapes should be systematically dubbed; only the copies should be used by the public
- Papers should be stored in acid-free folders, and photographic materials should be stored in archival preservers
- Tapes should be housed in proper containers and stored vertically on the shelves

Contracts

When archival records are deposited in an institution, a contract governing the use of that material should be signed by the institution and the depositor, taking into account any previous agreements between collector and informant(s). Depositing fieldwork data might involve the legal transfer of property. As in any transfer of title, it is necessary for the archives accepting this material to be assured that the title is clear - that the materials truly are the depositor's. Agreements may be made to allow public access to the material, or to restrict use until a later date, when access would be more appropriate. Restrictions are often necessary to accommodate the collector/depositor's pending research, dissertation, or publication, or to protect informants for political or personal reasons. Remember that deposit in an institution today often means possible dissemination on the Internet. Check what mechanisms are in place to protect holdings if they are mounted on the Web and make it clear in the contract whether Web (or other digital) access is permissible.

Access to collections

Once your fieldwork data has been accessioned by an institution, access to that data should be provided by that institution in one or more of the following formats:

- Collection description/summary
- Finding aid
- Index
- In-house database
- National bibliographic database
- Library catalog

You will play a role in this process both directly and indirectly. If your notes and annotations are detailed and clear, staff can efficiently process and catalog your collection. In some cases, however, it may be necessary for you to provide additional information. The accessibility of your field collection will be only as complete as the information you provide.

V

Post-deposit maintenance

Don't forget about your collections once they are safely deposited in an institution. Always make sure the institution has current contact details for you so that your collection can be properly administered.

Also, make a point to notify the institution if you publish papers/books relating to the material deposited. This will help keep your collection updated and cross-referenced.

Finally, think what you would like to happen to the administration of your collection after your death and let the institution know of your intentions. You may need to provide for any royalties to be paid out to informants, or you may wish to transfer all copyrights you hold to the archiving institution. Remember that it costs archives to preserve your materials and you may be able to repay them in some fashion by granting them your copyrights. But again, only do this if you have carefully written guidelines for the use of your materials.

Ethical Considerations

The following document was approved by the Board of the Society for Ethnomusicology in 1998. As these "Ethical Considerations" will be reviewed periodically, SEM members are encouraged to comment on details of the text as well as on the general utility of the document. Send comments to Beverley Diamond, Chair, SEM Ethics Committee, bdiamond@yorku.ca

I. General

A. The Society for Ethnomusicology, by addressing ethical concerns, hopes to stimulate ongoing dialogue and debate in order to gain increased understanding of ethical perspectives, and thus to respond as necessary to ethical issues in the changing discipline of ethnomusicology.

B. The Society for Ethnomusicology acknowledges that ethical systems differ among ethnomusicologists and that the ethical values affirmed by these statements do not necessarily represent those of all practitioners of ethnomusicology everywhere.

C. The Society for Ethnomusicology also acknowledges that ethical systems and values may differ between ethnomusicologists and their field consultants.

D. These statements therefore serve as a formal acknowledgment of shared ethical standards of our profession. They recognize common ground while respecting differences in experience and perspective.

II. Field Research

As one of the human sciences, ethnomusicology has a particular responsibility to deal ethically with the people and communities that work with ethnomusicologists.

A. Responsible conduct in field research in ethnomusicology is guided by the following obligations:

- Honesty in the representation of oneself and one's work.

- Cultivation of relationships based on informed consent, rights of privacy and confidentiality, and mutual respect.

- Sensitivity to other cultures' and individuals' ethical values.

- Sensitivity to proprietary concerns regarding recorded materials, photographs, and other documentation.

- Awareness of the connection between proprietary concerns and economic interests, as well as anticipation of future conflicts that may be caused by one's research activities.

B. Ethnomusicologists acknowledge that the responsibilities of field research extend beyond the fieldwork setting and often involve a long-term commitment to the rights and concerns of field consultants and their communities.

C. Ethnomusicologists acknowledge that field research may create or contribute to the basic conditions for future unanticipated, possibly exploitative, uses of recordings and other documentation. They recognize responsibility for their part in these processes and seek ways to prevent and/or address misuse of such materials when appropriate.

D. Ethnomusicologists recognize the need to be informed regarding copyright and other laws pertaining to the ownership of intellectual and cultural property and to be aware of the potential protections and liabilities of contractual arrangements dealing with depositing, licensing, and distributing musical sound and audiovisual recordings.

III. Publication

Ethnomusicologists acknowledge their responsibility to share research data and findings through publication via various media, and, in these endeavors, to continue to maintain confidentiality agreements as well as give credit to consultants, colleagues, students, and others where appropriate.

IV. Education

A. Ethnomusicologists accept their role as educators in both formal and informal teaching and training settings and, in their teaching, endeavor to include information about and discussion of ethical issues, particularly regarding field research.

B. Ethnomusicologists accept the necessity of preparing students and trainees to make informed judgments regarding ethical matters in field situations, by making sure they acquire sufficient knowledge to understand the social, cultural, political, economic, and legal realities of the communities in which they plan to work, as well as the potential impact of the processes and products of their work.

BIBLIOGRAPHY

Bartis, Peter. *Folklife and Fieldwork: A Layman's Introduction to Field Techniques* (Publications of the American Folklife Center, no. 3). Washington, D.C.: American Folklife Center, 1990.

Briggs, Charles L. *Learning How to Ask: A Sociolinguistic Appraisal of the Role of the Interview in Social Science Research* (Studies in the Social and Cultural Foundations of Language No. 1). New York: Cambridge University Press, 1986.

Dyal, Susan. *Preserving Traditional Arts: A Toolkit for Native American Communities*. Los Angeles: American Indian Studies Center, University of California, 1985.

Ives, Edward D. *The Tape-Recorded Interview: A Manual for Field Workers in Folklore and Oral History*. Knoxville: University of Tenessee Press, 1980.

Jackson, Bruce. *Fieldwork*. Urbana: University of Illinois Press, 1987.

Kensworthy, Mary Anne, Eleanor M. King, Mary Elizabeth Ruwell, and Trudy Van Houton. *Preserving Field Records: Archival Techniques for Archaeologists and Anthropologists*. Philadelphia: The University Museum, 1985.

Nettl, Bruno. *The Study of Ethnomusicology: Twenty-Nine Issues and Concepts*. Urbana: University of Illinois Press, 1983.

VII

Reimer, Derek. *Voices: A Guide to Oral History*. Province of British Columbia, 1984.

Sanjek, Roger, ed. *Fieldnotes: The Makings of Anthropology*. Ithaca: Cornell University Press, 1990.

Sinacore-Guinn, David. *Collective Administration of Copyright and Neighbouring Rights: International Practices, Procedures, and Organizations*. Boston, Toronto, London: Little, Brown and Company, 1993.

Schüller, Dietrich. "Minidisc in the Field? Applying Archiving Principles to Data Gathering" *IASA Journal* 14:35–40 (December 1999).

Seeger, Anthony. "The Role of Sound Archives in Ethnomusicology Today, " *Ethnomusicology* 30 (2): 261–76 (Spring/Summer 1986).

Stewart, Stephen M. *International Copyright and Neighbouring Rights*. London, Boston, Dublin, etc.: Butterworth's, 1993.

Ward, Alan. *A Manual of Sound Archive Adminstration*. Hampshire, England: Gower, 1990.

White, Glenn. *The Audio Dictionary* (2nd Edition). Seattle: University of Washington Press, 1991.

Wilson, William A. "Documenting Folklore," in *Folk Groups and Folklore Genres: An Introduction*, Elliot Oring, ed. Logan, Utah: Utah State University Press, 1986, 225-54.

The World Intellectual Property Organization. *Introduction to Intellectual Property Theory and Practice.* London, The Hague, Boston: Kluwer International, 1997.

Internet Sources

DAT information:
    www.solorb.com/dat-heads/

MiniDisc information:
    www.minidisc.org/

Microphone information
    www.harmony-central.com/Other/mic-faq.txt

Digital photography information:
    www.imaging-resource.com
    www.dcresource.com/faq/faq.html

Motion picture information:
    www.redballoon.net/~snorwood/faq2.

Video information:
    www.cybercollege.com/tvp047.htm
    betacam.palsite.com/format.html
    www.dvcentral.org/dvwhat.html

External power supply information:
    www.bescor.com/
    www.ecocharge.com

VII